Foolproof

Heart

Foolproof Heart

Michelle Gochett Edwards

Foolproof Heart
Copyright © 2019 Michelle Gochett Edwards

ISBN:
978-0-9998534-2-9

Library of Congress Control Number:
2021907638

Printed in the United States of America.

Dedicated to my Mama,
who anticipated everything
in her teachings.
Your love and wisdom
led me home.

Contents

This book is for anyone who's ever been fooled.
Whether you're immersed in a toxic relationship
or recovering from the fallout,
"Foolproof Heart" provides clarity,
empowerment and wisdom to sustain you.

Perhaps you recently unmasked
the monster in your life masquerading
as a soulmate, fake friend or family member.
Maybe you're looking for a reminder
on the importance of self-love and
how it can protect you from unnecessary pain.

No matter what your situation, "Foolproof Heart"
will give you words of wisdom to take
on your life journey.
Remember, we're all fooled by someone
or something, but not forever and hopefully
not for long.

Unmasking

Dare I resurrect
the dead?
The ghost still lodged in my head.
Whose lies still fill me with dread.
My broken heart,
the constant thread.
Or, should I think a few moves ahead
and let the dirty dog
sleep instead?

Wake him up!

Drifter, drifter
coming through.
On the beat,
into my purview.
The man, the man,
wearing dark blue.
Piercing eyes,
that see through you.
So polite, saying please,
but it's all a tease
before you're on your knees.
A twisted play to make you pay
for all the pain
that calls his name.

- *drifter*

When you met me,
I was vulnerable.
Weak.
My winning streak,
bleak.
And on that fateful street,
you swept me off my feet.

- *prey*

Your smile,
that **brazen** confidence,
was a beacon.
Undeniable and irresistible.
My defenses lowered.
A curiosity aroused.

- *attraction*

You disguise your
icy heart
in bravado and bravery.
Trustee of
endangered hearts,
a member of the cavalry.
Your gift is pretending you care
as you plunge souls into despair.
Few find out how cold you are until
they're firmly confined in your snare.

- *cold-blooded*

It didn't feel
like a trap.
You, reading my mind,
knowing my thoughts ahead of time.
Feeding me your reliable and
infallible elixir - love.
The words,
"*I love you*,"
get them every time.
It got me.

- *love bombing*

It feels warm and safe
basking in your spotlight.
Bathing in your shine.
Drowning in your compliments.
Your eyes on me, only me.
I'm so happy.
Alive.
Lucky, that a divine hand crosses our paths.
This is destiny.
We are soulmates,
the beginning of forever.

- *crush*

I can't see where
I'm going.
We're moving fast,
you're in a hurry.
"Relax baby,"
you tell me.
"I've got you.
Don't worry."
Your attention overwhelms me.
I'm falling in love with you.
Intoxicated by the sweetest wine,
your lies,
fresh off the vine.

- *falling*

You condition me.
Test my boundaries.
See how far you can go.
What I accept.
When I say no.
Pull me toward you.
Push me away.
Reward and punish.
Titillate and tease.
Bend my will to yours.

I follow you,
seeing the inconsistencies,
but ignoring,
rationalizing,
desiring only to remain
in your magnetic glow.

- grooming

You're heavy.
Draining.
An unsolvable mystery,
I want to solve.
I'm invested and once
I'm in your arms,
I'm hooked.
The thought of letting you go
feels heavier.

- *weight*

There's darkness in you that attracts
and repels.
When I'm not careful,
I fall completely
under your spell.

That's what you do,
cast spells.
Get people drunk
off a taste of you.

I like the way
you taste
on my tongue.

- *spellbound*

You lure me in playing
the role of gentleman,
then introduce me to your savage.
Calling us "we," you
describe the things
you'll do to me.
Prologue.
Acts.
Epilogue.
Volumes one, two
and three.

- *foreplay*

I ride you,
full throttle.
Speeding through
the cautions
until I'm
wrecked.

- addicted to the danger

I never knew
deceptiveness
could exist in a kiss
disguised
as
bliss.

- your kiss is dark magic

Sex
is not how I imagine or dream.
The one thing you promise,
the one thing that lures me in
is always missing…
love.

- *missing*

You don't notice my
hesitation or trepidation.
The growing regret
of accepting these invitations.
I go through the motions,
hoping love shows up.
It doesn't.
Instead, I'm a prop
in your perverted workshop.

Devoid of emotion,
a checklist of positions
you silently cross off.
There's no closeness,
only distance.
Pushing inside me,
your tongue plunging down my throat,
you've never felt
f u r t h e r
away.

This is not love.

- *you're a liar*

Facing the truth
feels unbearable
and I run from it for a long time,
though the truth always
catches up with me.

The truth lying next to me,
growing colder, more impatient
by the minute.
I desperately want
to cleave,
but you desire most
to leave.

- *time's up*

I don't sleep after you go.
My body, on high alert,
listening out for you.
There's the ding of the nearby elevator.
The commotion of another guest
entering their room.
Hours later, I'm still waiting… for you.
The words "*be right back*" lingering
like a suffocating cloud over the dark room.

The only movement,
a candle flickering and my heart.
My heart, a growing hysterical beat.
I'm unable to move from the bed,
your scent taunting me on the sheets.
It fills the room, your cologne.
I text and you don't answer,
but I see you online and
the tears flow and I accept it.
You're
not
coming
back.

- *broken*

I try to believe
it's beautiful when
we're shrouded in candlelight.
But every time
morning arrives,
the
ugliness
shines.

 - *after*

The sunrise,
this brilliant light,
is a welcome gift from your darkness.
My eyes are puffy and tired.
You're not supposed to cry for hours on end.
I rise, shower and begin to curl my hair.
The phone vibrates.
It's you.
"Good morning,"
you write.
I'm happy.
I'm sad.
I'm angry.
I'm disrespected.
I'm used, dead and resurrected.
I should ignore you after how you've treated me.
But instead I surrender the last vestiges
of my self-respect and text back,
"good morning."

- surrendering

I try to hold on to you,
while losing
grip of myself.
Trying again and again
to recapture what was present
in the beginning.
Enduring indignities and hostilities.
It's clear your attention
is diverting elsewhere.

- *desperation*

It's your birthday and I plan a trip.
One, you decide to skip.
A decision you keep hidden until the end.
I'm waiting at the gate,
wondering why you're running late.
I call and you answer right away.
You say, "sorry for the delay,
traffic's bad on the highway
but don't worry, I'll be with you in a sec."
You tell me, "baby, board the flight,
there's something special for you tonight,"
but my instincts tell me something isn't right.

The final boarding call arrives
and there's no you, only your lies.
Your phone goes to voicemail right away.
A brutal punishment aimed at my diminishment.
Why am I taking this?
There's no replenishing it.

On my way home, you're blowing up my phone,
sending text, after text, after text.
My mind is perplexed, at your cruel,
disordered flex.
I wonder what new low will come next.

- *savage*

Your abandonment
leaves me sick.
I'm inconsolable.
Suffering from mental blow after blow.
Still, I don't go.
Participant in every new low.
Dismissing all that I know.
Believing false promises of tomorrow.

Enduring the mean,
to sample the sweet.
This "*love*" you dangle
is just a treat,
you parcel out
to prevent retreat.

- *manipulations*

First, I'm loved
then I'm hated.
My worth devalued,
then inflated.
Ruse after ruse,
feeling more and more confused.
But there's one fact I can't refuse.
The cause of
each and every painful
bruise … is you.

Narcissist

Confronted with
the truth, all the evidence,
all the proof,
I see you
for the first time.
All I let pass,
now a thousand shards
of glass.
But in the shattering,
some vivid clarity.

- *clarity*

You can rationalize and make
excuses to deny what
you're experiencing
and seeing.
But until you accept
the monster before you,
you're going to continue to get
p u m m e l e d.

- *realities*

What **darkness** exists in you
allowing you to do what you do?
This shadow that prevents you from being true
to the ones devoted to you.
A craving, a yearning to dominate,
mistreat, mislead, discriminate.
No rules, just games.
No love, just hate and
only you decide when to placate.

Inside your ego is churning,
your instincts simply burning.
The constant feed to fill your needs,
the attractions just keep coming.

Alone with you is demeaning.
No connection, no real feeling.
Souls leave stunned and reeling.
But one day your games will end.
The world will conspire to extinguish your fire
and your license to hurt will expire.

- dark

The **blessing** in disguise.
The day you open your eyes.
The façade falls.
Self-love calls.
The mask slips and
the monster loses its grip.

- *released*

We can tolerate many things
when love is present.
Rough hands don't always
hurt us where they land.
A cross word doesn't get you banned.
But when love is missing in an
intimate relationship, there is often
bad intention and
even worse treatment.

- *devastated*

Telling someone
you *love* them
is a declaration of war…
when it's
a lie.

Sometimes "*love*"
is the lie
you tell yourself,
in order to endure
something
you shouldn't.

- *war-torn*

Nursing my blues,
for missing
the clues.
Oh, how
regrets
o o z e.

- regrets

"*Give me another chance*," you say,
months later.
Your reappearance, via text.
"You want *another chance*
to finish me off."
"**No**," I say,
"I've come too far to let you break
me again."

- *no more chances*

You try another mask.
"I miss you,
I still love you," you say.
Struggling to reconcile
this softer version before me,
flashbacks flood my mind
in rapid succession.
Is this the same man
who taught me
the harsh lessons?

- *split*

I want you.
I don't want you back.
I want you.
I don't want you back.
I can **never** go back.
You don't want me back.

I want me back.

You left me broken.
Not even a token.
No words spoken.
You aren't a lover.
You're a hater.
A brutal traitor.
Smooth operator.
A **bomber**
with a detonator.

- *bomber*

Everything
was deliberate:
every *move*,
every *word*.
Some people calculate
every *wound*
they make.

- *calculated*

I waste time worrying what you
think of me.
The hard lesson is you
don't think
any less of me.
You don't think of me
at all.

- disposable

I sped like a meteorite,
straight into you.
Crashing.
Burning.
Destroying everything,
but mostly myself.
A brilliant display of
self-destruction.

- *self-destructive*

You create
a beautiful
fiction, that's
how you
fuel addictions.

- fictitious

You convince me
we're a special kind
of magic and
I believe it,
until I realize
that's the trick.

- *tricked*

That our demise
doesn't devastate you,
bring you to your knees,
make you beg
p l e a s e,
helps me seize the keys
and leave.

- and you let me go

The goal was to *have*
but never to hold
because some
hearts are counterfeit,
not gold.

- *fake*

Some men
can have you
again and again because
of how they make you feel.

And some men
will never have you again
because of how they
made you feel.

- never again

And then there was nothing.
Not the sound of
your voice
or boom of your laughter.
Only the torturous beat of my heart
trying to forget you.

- *disposable*

Some occasions
are commemorated.
Other dates are
unstated,
weighted
and complicated
like the day I met you.

- it's complicated

It's inevitable from its inception,
a failing at its very conception.
Connections ignited in deception,
ultimately end in rejection
and deep introspection.
There's nary an exception.

- *consequences*

The final decision,
after many long,
tortured deliberations
inside my head.
A decision to act,
after so long paralyzed.
The heart desiring
not to sting or bruise.
The mind screaming loudly,
"off with the head."
A compromise.
No more acknowledgement.
No more words.
You are not worthy
of any more words.

- we don't speak

When I know you
will feast on my pain,
only one option
remains…
to let you **starve**.

- *no contact*

And then,
just as cruelly as you,
I crumpled up
our memories
and threw you away too.

- done

Recovering

I bury you,
then dig you up,
day after day.
I must live to
no longer give you
life.

- caretaker

My loved ones have been searching for me
for months.
Worried, because I have been missing.
My normal effervescent self, lost.
Rising from another failed attempt,
my determination to leave here is steadfast.
I will not die here.
I will not wither away in your maze of confusion.
This once alluringly, mysterious place
is suffocating.
It's dark, thorny and dangerous.
You laugh as I run for my life,
but I'm resolute.
I will not lose myself like so many others.
I will return to the people who love me.
I will return whole.

- depression

There are times
your presence still looms so large,
the darkest clouds or
sudden gusts of wind
and yet you're not here.
But in my memory,
I find a new offense,
some punishing consequence
of my time with you.

- *demons*

Like ripples in a current,
you come and go.
First, motion sickness
and thickness
then, home sickness.

- *queasy*

But you were never
my home.
You were a squatter
and only
I can clean up
the mess you left.

- *evicted*

You filled
what I thought
was an empty space
in my life.
But when you left,
I realized the
only thing
that was empty
was you.
I was always full.
I just didn't know it.

- *empty*

Away from you,
parts of me emerge
that I never knew existed.
Enlisted and assisted
by your twisted existence.
You persisted,
but I resisted.

- resistance

You've got to revel
in the silence,
I tell myself.
Feel empowered marooned
on the island alone.
Standing up for yourself
often ignites a vengeful response
from those used to taking advantage of you.
Sit in your power
and say …
no more.

- *no more*

To heal,
I supply myself…
with words.
Strengthening my resolve,
gives breath to my rage,
inspiration to pour
onto the page.

- *supply*

Words give the
heartbreak meaning.
A way to express all the hurt
I'm feeling.
Writing helps me escape
and find healing.
Displaying the pain,
instead of concealing.
Gaining strength,
a higher power starts revealing.
The deception and trauma,
in which, I'm dealing.
That I can't follow
where it is you're leading.
A place where pain is all I'm receiving.
The only choice I have
is leaving.

- find what heals you

Though you're battered,
your heart in tatters,
the only thing that matters
is you did not shatter.

- strong

You will never heal.
You will never
move forward
until you stop
clinging to the fiction
and **accept the facts**.

- *facts*

Facts illuminate
the path to
understanding
and healing.
Unmasking
new revelations.

- epiphany

You reveal a *weakness*,
one I didn't see.
You got in because
I didn't love me.

- hard truths

There's a moment
in a relationship when
the big reveal happens.
A twisted heart shows
out in such a way that you can't overlook.
A grave character inconsistency
unmasked or a penetrating wound delivered.

When this happens, I hope you have
the strength and courage to believe
what you see and feel.
I pray you have enough self-love
to walk away, no matter
the time invested.

- brave

There are signs
everywhere you go.
Stop.
Go.
Slow.
People show
signs, too.
At the beginning of a relationship,
people are often on their best behavior.
Still, people who are going to be
a problem later
show signs early.
Learn to read
the signs
people show you
and act,
before attachment builds.
It may save your psyche.
It may save your life.

- *signs*

Consider yourself gifted
anytime a veil is lifted
and the darkness
once concealed
is revealed.

- *gifted*

My prayer is that you
find out the hidden,
the purposely disguised,
the soul-crushing surprise
before it leads to
your demise.

- *amen*

Looking back used to spark blame
and feelings of shame.
Now all I see is how much
I overcame and I'm proud
of how far I've come.

- *proud*

Breaking away
from toxic people
feels like breathing fresh air
after you've been suffocated.
You realize how
important it is
to breathe,
to keep breathing,
to keep moving forward.

- *breathe*

We haphazardly
give undeserving
and unproven people
the nuclear codes
to our entire universe;
our heart's terrain.
When they blow
us up,
we have the audacity
to ask how?
Why?

- *undeserving*

It's the injuries
you inflict upon yourself
that hurt the most,
even after distance
and healing.
The signs you ignored.
The intuition you
didn't follow.
Loving yourself means
choosing environments and people
that nurture, love and cherish you.
Once you truly love yourself,
a fool can't fool
you anymore.

- *foolproof*

You did not make
my soft places rough.
No matter
how hard you tried.

- *unsuccessful*

Empowering

The emotions eventually leave.
Those uncontrollable and sudden
bouts of regret and longing.
But **wisdom stays**
and you forgive yourself
for being played.

- wisdom

Acceptance and healing
eliminate the compulsion
to return to people who
mistreat you.
When you reach a deeper level
of reverence for yourself,
there's nothing
anyone can say or do
to entrap you.
Once fortified,
the healed version
of yourself won't allow
abuse again.

- *victorious*

It's not the heartbreak
that you focus on anymore,
it's the knowledge.
Not the destination,
but the journey
of self-discovery.

- *refocused*

Embrace that what you experienced
was no great love story.
Nothing to romanticize or revisit.
Accept that you were simply
an opportunity
someone took advantage of
and nothing more.

- *opportunistic*

Reserve nostalgia for
the parts of your life
that deserve it.
Not the parts you re-write
because they're too
painful to relive.

- *nostalgic*

Run,
if love shows up indifferent.
That's when it's most important
to listen because
love treats you
different.

- _run like hell_

Different means special.
Honoring your presence
with deeds.
Taking care of your physical
and emotional needs.
Planting good seeds.
Having the patience to see
what grows over time.

- *growth*

Temporary people
sometimes enter our lives
to force us to grow.
Their time with us is fleeting,
but their impact is everlasting.
We're not the same
after they leave.
We're not supposed to be.

- *changed*

Some journeys
are supposed to
break you,
shake your very core,
to underscore
the importance of
loving yourself more.

- *perspective*

Your worst moment
becomes the gritty foundation
you use to rebuild yourself.
The experience helping you realize
how much you didn't know,
how much you needed to grow.
Find your light and
never let go.

- hold onto the light

D i s t a n c e
gives you strength.
Strength
helps you
keep your *d i s t a n c e.*

- *distance*

You have some of the most
powerful tools
in your personal arsenal.
Intuition is one of them.
Listen to it.
Keep it sharp,
because the more you suppress it,
the duller it becomes.
When intuition becomes dull,
it malfunctions and
deactivates, normalizing behaviors
that should raise alarm.
Actions that, in the end,
cause you harm.

- *intuition*

Unless you surrender your
power, <u>no</u> <u>one</u> can
destroy your self-worth.
It's often the
people struggling
with their own feelings
of worthlessness
that try to tear you down.

Never cede your power.

Recognize there are
people suffering,
who would rather
hurt you, than heal themselves.

- only you have the power

Boundaries
are walls
that guard
important places.
Beware of climbers.

- *enforce your boundaries*

Love yourself so much,
you immediately and
decisively extract
people from your life
who rob you of your joy
and jeopardize
your mental health.

- prioritize yourself

You are the safe
you must crack.
The answers are
stored inside
for you to unpack.

- *safecracker*

The best person
to unwrap you,
is you.
Not the untested people coming
in and out of your life promising love.
Uncover and deal with the unhealed
and vulnerable
parts of yourself before
someone else
exploits them.

- *unwrap yourself*

Remember
you're **strong**,
even in your weakest moments.
Strength,
you have to own it.

- *own it*

You've got to be unabashed
about putting yourself
out there again.
Unmoved by judgment and derision.
Make a decision
to bring all of you!

- be yourself

Allow love
to chart your course and
do not traverse storms
for people who do not
love you.

- don't do it

Our desire to become two
often clouds our ability to see through.
The con artists, users and abusers
able to sense, target and devour you.
We contort ourselves trying to
fit into a carefully coordinated scam.
A "*love*" sham.
Shedding morals,
dismantling boundaries
and lowering our standards.
And how do we defend all that we upend?
We say, "*we thought it was love.*"

The traffickers of fake love will keep up
the "*I love you*" masquerade for eternity
if it gets them what they want: sex,
money and wasting your valuable time.
Your reputation maligned,
and spirit resigned.
Leave him or her behind
and save your mind.

- master the art of leaving

Searching for love can leave
you war-weary
and defeated.
Your heart, depleted.
But remain positive.
Resilient.
Open to new possibilities.
Don't give up until
you find the love you
deserve and the love
that deserves you.

- don't give up

Before rewarding
your flesh,
first, consider
the damage
to your soul.

- your soul matters most

Constant and
over the top
declarations of love
early in a relationship
can signal many things:
insecurity, deception,
possessiveness and manipulation.
None of which have anything
to do with love.

- *red flags*

Love fulfills promises,
reinforcing words
with actions.
There's no ambivalence
or hidden mystery
because you are
a certainty.

- *love is certain about you*

We're all looking
for the same things.
A warm place
out of the cold.
A heart to hold.
To exit this love race
with someone
to grow old.

- *goals*

Self-love is the gate,
the guard,
the sniper…
that keeps
you safe.

- *your love tops all*

In life's apothecary,
there are many drugs you can choose:

-gratification
-denial
-retaliation
-subjugation

The best cure-all is loving yourself.
It, alone, offers immunity against those who don't
have your best interests at heart.

- self-love gives you immunity

Vote for yourself.
Stand up for yourself.
Love yourself.
Take care of yourself.
Protect yourself.
If you're not important to yourself,
you won't be to anyone else.

- it begins and ends with you

Back with a vengeance,
uncompromising and inflexible.
Its re-emergence,
the result of deep introspection,
examination, and healing
after being discarded,
abused and used.
**A realization that you, and
only you, are your best protector**.
The only one to dictate
how you're treated.
Vow to never again
sacrifice your
self-respect.

- *respect yourself*

Don't accept scraps,
leftovers,
limited availability,
temporary parking,
a short-term investment or any
position other than number one.

- *standards*

Your parting gift is
the newfound ability to see
through the subterfuge.
No matter how lonely it may get,
never put on your blinders again.
Accept this gift of insight.
Use it to rebuild your life
and love again.

- move forward with wisdom

Repeat after me.

"Let this journey
herald a new me,
distinctly free
from who and what
I used to be.
Found finally at
the place
of loving me."

- *free*

Make a resolution
to love because every
good thing in life
springs from there.
Love those who love you, hard.
But **love yourself harder**
because that will
make all the difference.

- resolutions

Look deeper into the person
staring back at you in the mirror.
You're a survivor.
Indestructible.
Your future, bright.
Your indomitable spirit, ready for flight.

Freed from a harrowing experience,
your beauty and strength remain.
That light, refusing to darken.
That fight, having won the battle within.
No one can stop you now.

- the best is yet to come

You are not a plot point on a map.
A temporary layover.
A place to visit, but not stay.
You embody
the beauty
of an undiscovered country.
Full of rolling hills and valleys,
not yet explored.
Vast resources, untapped.
Mysteries, still unsolved.
Some lucky person
will call you home.

- your love is home

I hope you find love.
The kind of love,
not challenged by a shorter skirt
or six-pack.
Not put in jeopardy by youth
or boredom.
But the kind of love
that is as guaranteed
as a new day and
as sure as nightfall.
Love that sustains and remains
for as long as it is written.

- *true love*

Hopefully the poems in "Foolproof Heart" remind
you that you possess a heart that is
precious and priceless.
But most importantly, it's my hope that these words
reinforce that the onus is on <u>you</u> to protect your
heart, mind, body and soul.

There's a reason why self-love is important.
Why its necessity is championed in pulpits,
movies, books and memes.
Self-love helps you avoid and release yourself from
experiences and people that will
hurt and sometimes destroy you.

When we love ourselves, we don't give away our
power and willingly subject ourselves to pain.
We trust our instincts about people.

Loving yourself won't exempt you from pain,
but it will help you develop a "Foolproof Heart."
Your presence is a gift and when it's not
appreciated, honored and celebrated,
take it back.

Love,
Michelle